on the motorway
SPY IT! SCORE IT!

Introduction

The first motorway to be completed in Britain was the Preston bypass, which subsequently became the M6. It was just eight miles long and opened in December 1958. Next came the first motorway to be built with three-lane carriageways; this was the 72-mile stretch of the London–Yorkshire M1 between Aldenham and Crick, which opened 11 months later. By January 1972, the first 1000 miles of motorway had been completed. Motorways have come a long way since those early days and the volume of traffic that uses them has increased beyond anyone's imagination.

Even though motorways have helped speed journeys up considerably, for passengers, a long motorway journey can be very boring. Not any longer with i-SPY On the Motorway! It is surprising how much there is to see along the way. But whatever you do, do not distract the driver – he or she must concentrate on driving.

How to use your i-SPY book

Keep your eyes peeled for the i-SPYs in the book.

If you spy it, score it by ticking the circle or star.

Items with a star are difficult to spot so you'll have to search high and low to find them.

Once you score 1000 points, send away for your super i-SPY certificate. Follow the instructions on page 64 to find out how.

Joining the motorway

Traffic lights

Traffic lights control vehicles at junctions to allow free-flowing traffic and to help avoid jams.

5 POINTS

Slip road

Slip roads allow motorists to safely reach motorway speed before joining the main carriageway.

5 POINTS

No entry sign

Stop! Do not go along this road – cars will be coming the other way.

5 POINTS

Start of motorway sign

After this point, motorway rules apply.

5 POINTS

Joining the motorway

Blue motorway sign

All motorway signs are made in this special blue colour.

Green primary route sign

These are for main or A roads all around the country...

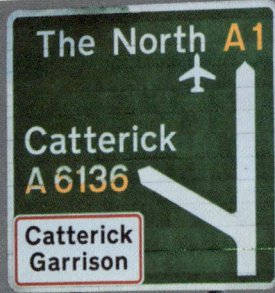

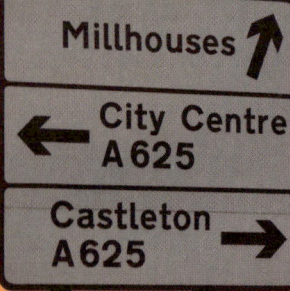

White local route sign

...and these are used for local roads.

Chevrons

5 POINTS

This sign is a warning to drivers of a sharp bend ahead.

Lanes joining

You may need to go around a long curve, known as a slip road, to join the motorway.

10 POINTS

Roadmarkings

10 POINTS

Destinations painted on lanes give drivers clear information to help them pass through a junction.

Lanes and carriageways

Three lanes

Most motorways in Britain are three lanes wide.

Two lanes

Some have less traffic so only need two lanes...

Four lanes

...but some carry so much traffic at the busiest times that they need four lanes to help avoid jams.

Hard shoulder

Traffic is not permitted on the hard shoulder, except in case of breakdown or when instructed.

5 POINTS

Motorway splits

Major junctions where motorways split in different directions often have signs for two miles before.

5 POINTS

No hard shoulder

Some motorways have limited space and do not have any room for a hard shoulder.

10 POINTS

Motorways merge from left

Watch out, merging motorway traffic will be moving very quickly.

5 POINTS

Lanes and carriageways

Junction

A motorway junction is spread out over almost half a mile. The entry and exit slip roads allow time for drivers to accelerate to and slow down from motorway speeds.

Steel central barrier

The central barrier in the middle of the motorway is a safety feature to help prevent cars travelling in opposite directions from hitting each other.

100-metres markers

These markers are placed every 100 metres.

Cat's eyes

Cat's eyes were invented by a man from Halifax in 1933 when he noticed the tram lines set in the road were shining in the sunlight, making the road look like lanes. Every time a car runs over one it 'cleans' the eye.

Concrete central barrier

These concrete barriers stop much bigger vehicles like trucks and coaches and are much safer.

Signs

Crosswind warning sign

There could be strong crosswinds in exposed areas such as bridges or on high ground.

Brown tourist sign

These brown signs are for tourist information.

Direction sign

This sign gives drivers information about the next junctions. They are usually found up to a mile before the exit.

Triangle – warning

Triangular signs give warnings about hazards.

Round – order

Round signs give orders that you must obey.

Rectangle – information

These rectangular signs give information.

Signs

Distance on motorway

It is important to know how far it is to your destination.

5 POINTS

Ferry sign

Take this route for the ferry.

10 POINTS

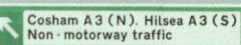

Airport sign

And this one for the airport.

10 POINTS

Slow lorries

This is a warning sign. Going up a hill is likely to slow heavy lorries down.

10 POINTS

County border

At this point you are passing into a new county.

Services

This sign tells you the next services area is one mile away.

Works unit only

Only authorised vehicles are allowed beyond this point.

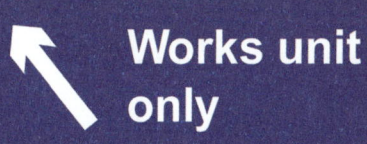

Variable message signs

Variable message signs give instant information about the dangers that may be ahead.

Fog

In poor visibility conditions such as fog, drivers need to be warned to slow down.

10 POINTS

Speed limits

Because of a high volume of traffic, the speed limit has been reduced to 50 mph.

10 POINTS

Strong winds

Strong winds are particularly dangerous to high-sided vehicles so HGV drivers should be cautious.

10 POINTS

Don't drive tired

Accidents can be caused by drivers who fall asleep at the wheel. Don't drive tired – take a break.

10 POINTS

Freezing conditions

If the temperature drops, look out for this sign.

Salt spreading

The salt and grit spread by gritting lorries helps keep the roads from freezing but it can be distracting if you drive past one without a warning.

Keep left

When driving on the motorway, drivers should always keep to the left unless they are overtaking another vehicle.

Variable message signs

Drive with care

Caution, drive with care – there may be danger ahead.

10 POINTS

Speed/distance indicator

This sign lets drivers know how far it is until a specific junction.

10 POINTS

Vehicles

Truck cab

Sometimes, cabs are between jobs and travel without their trailers.

10 POINTS

Tanker truck

Tanker trucks deliver fuel to garages and fuel stations, but they also deliver other liquids, like milk.

10 POINTS

Container truck

Containers, holding lots of products, can be moved around the world (usually by sea), moving from one truck to another.

10 POINTS

Vehicles

Car transporter

This car transporter is delivering new vehicles to showrooms.

5 POINTS

Box trailer

This box trailer is delivering food to a supermarket. There are often adverts on the side of these trailers.

5 POINTS

Curtain side truck

A curtain side truck is really useful if you need to get to something right at the back. It's easy to load one with a fork lift truck from the side.

5 POINTS

Army truck

The army transports all sorts of people and equipment with this general purpose truck. Army trucks are almost always green, have huge tyres and can travel over rough terrain, but you often see one on the motorway too.

40 POINTS

TOP SPOT!

Vehicles

Oversize load/convoy exceptionale

Even houses need to be transported sometimes. This mobile home is not heavy but it is too large for a normal truck. Look out for an 'oversize load' or 'convoy exceptionale'.

25 POINTS

Low-loader

This low-loader trailer can haul very heavy weights, like large construction machines, and keep the centre of gravity low to the ground, reducing the risk of it toppling over.

10 POINTS

Coach

This coach is comfortable and has around 50 seats. Some even have tea and coffee available and a toilet.

Minibus

This minibus seats around 18 people. Many schools use a bus like this one.

Motorhome

The ideal vehicle to take on an adventure!

Vehicles

Car towing a caravan

The speed limit on the motorway is 70 mph, but if you are towing, it is 60 mph.

10 POINTS

Car towing a boat

When towing a boat, you have to make sure it is not too heavy for the tow vehicle.

20 POINTS

Van

This type of van is used to deliver smaller loads. See how many white ones you can see.

5 POINTS

Crane

This crane can lift around 35 tons, but some mobile cranes can lift up to 500 tons. That's 500 Ford Focus cars!

15 POINTS

Custom car

People spend thousands of pounds customising their cars so they can have them just how they want them.

20 POINTS

Highway maintenance vehicle

Motorways are in constant need of maintenance and repair and these trucks often work at night to reduce congestion.

10 POINTS

Vehicles

Breakdown van

If your car breaks down, the driver should call for roadside assistance. They will help repair the car so you can continue your journey.

10 POINTS

Breakdown recovery

If the vehicle cannot be repaired at the roadside, a breakdown recovery truck will take the vehicle and all of the passengers to a garage.

 15 POINTS

Motorbike

Ideal for avoiding traffic jams.

 **5 POINTS**

Hazard info

Look out for these hazard signs, they denote what type of load is being carried.

Biohazard

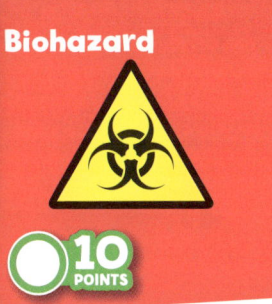

10 POINTS

Compressed gas

10 POINTS

Corrosive

10 POINTS

Oxidising

10 POINTS

Poison

10 POINTS

Radiation

10 POINTS

On the motorway

Overhead steel gantry holding signs

These need to hold many signs, often a sign for each lane. They are really useful for the driver if the carriageway is splitting into different directions.

 5 POINTS

Phone masts

All mobile phone companies have their masts by the motorway because a lot of people use these roads and need a good signal for their phones.

 10 POINTS

Crash protection truck

These high-visibility vehicles warn drivers of what is ahead.

 20 POINTS

Street lighting

In areas that are very busy, street lighting is often used to help improve visibility at night.

5 POINTS

Broken down car

If you break down, stand in a safe place behind the crash protection barrier.

10 POINTS

Tollbooths

Some motorways are not paid for by road taxes and drivers have to pay at a tollbooth to use them.

10 POINTS

SOS phones

If you should break down, drivers can use these SOS phones to call for help. They are marked with a unique number so emergency services know where to send assistance.

5 POINTS

On the motorway

Cutting

Acres of ancient grassland were lost to create this 1000 m long cutting at Twyford in Hampshire. Many people protested about the impact building this motorway would have, but despite this, its construction went ahead.

Noise absorbent barrier

 **5 POINTS**

The design of this fence helps to absorb the noise from the vehicles on the carriageway.

Embankment

To avoid motorways having too many hills, the carriageway can be built on a series of bridges, cuttings and embankments.

 **20 POINTS**

From the motorway

There are many things to see from the motorway – see how many of these you can spot before you get to your destination.

Tractor

You will be able to find tractors all year round. This one is ploughing a field...

10 POINTS

Combine harvester

...but this combine harvester is only used in the summer to gather in the crops.

10 POINTS

Cows

This cow does not seem to mind the noisy vehicles passing by.

5 POINTS

Pigs

15 POINTS

These piglets are having fun playing with each other.

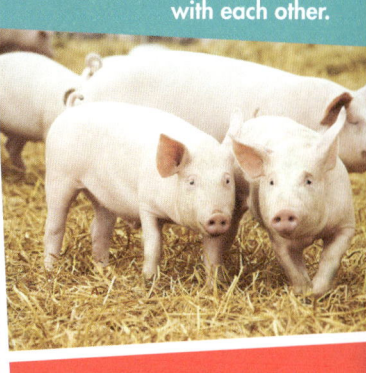

Ponies

These ponies keep the grass nice and short...

5 POINTS

Sheep

5 POINTS

...and so do the sheep.

From the motorway

Wind turbine

These wind turbines help produce clean energy – many can be seen from motorways, especially in remote areas.

5 POINTS

Power station

Watch out for the steam from the cooling towers.

10 POINTS

Pylons

Power lines are sometimes routed alongside motorways and main roads.

5 POINTS

Rivers

 **5 POINTS**

Rivers were once the transport highways for moving goods around the country.

Ferry port

Some ferries can carry 650 cars or 100 trucks, and hold over 2000 passengers.

 **10 POINTS**

Railway train

If you travel by rail next time, you could use i-SPY On a Train Journey! Many motorways are built next to railway lines.

 **5 POINTS**

From the motorway

Football ground

At home games, it's very noisy here and it's likely there will be a lot of traffic...

Hot-air balloon

...but it will be very peaceful here.

Castle

This is Windsor Castle, which can just about be seen from the M4 motorway, in the county of Berkshire. It has been the home for many of Britain's kings and queens for almost 1000 years.

25 POINTS

Refuel and take a break

There are more than a hundred motorway service stations in the UK. Watford Gap service area was the first of its kind, opening at the same time as the M1 on 2 November 1959.

Services sign

This is one of the signs that informs drivers that the services are approaching.

Ferrybridge services ½m

With access to all routes

Main building

This is the main services building where you can take a break and get refreshments.

Parent and child parking

5 POINTS

These parking bays are close to the building so they have been reserved for parents with children. You might also see parking spaces for blue badge holders that are also near the buildings for ease of access.

Car park junction

Car parks have a lot of vehicles moving around that need to be controlled.

5 POINTS

Outside seating

If the weather is good, you could sit outside and enjoy the fresh air and sunshine.

5 POINTS

Refuel and take a break

Food bar

While you are at the services, you may want a sandwich and a drink... **5 POINTS**

Restaurant

...or perhaps you have time to sit down and enjoy a meal in the restaurant. **5 POINTS**

People shopping

Most services have shops selling all kinds of things. **5 POINTS**

Picnic area

If you have brought along your own picnic, you could sit outside in the sunshine. **5 POINTS**

Waste bin

Keep the area tidy: put your waste in here.

 5 POINTS

Children's play area

Let off some steam at the play area.

5 POINTS

Refuel and take a break

Fuel station

The driver may need to refuel the car at the fuel station.

◯ **10 POINTS**

Fuel price sign

But check the price per litre is not too high first.

◯ **10 POINTS**

Unleaded Litre
142.5

Diesel Litre
144.0

Roadworks

Roads do not last forever! Every year the government spends millions of pounds on maintenance, repairs and improvements on the motorway network.

Arrow right

At this point, keep right.

10 POINTS

Cones

Some large sites use many thousands of cones over miles of roadworks.

5 POINTS

Delays possible

Wherever there are roadworks, there are usually delays.

10 POINTS

Roadworks

Average speed camera

These average speed cameras read the number plate of vehicles and measure their speed over a long distance. Driving too fast through roadworks is very unsafe and could result in a fine.

5 POINTS

Average speed sign

Motorists are warned about average speed cameras and to stay within the speed limit.

5 POINTS

Works access sign

This is a works site entrance giving access to workers' vehicles only.

5 POINTS

Diggers

10 POINTS

Track diggers like this one are often used on roadworks so that the work can be carried out with the minimum of delay.

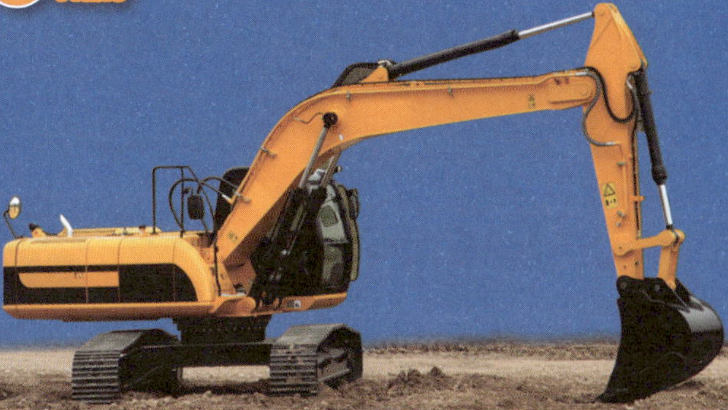

Road rollers

The ideal vehicle for making a perfectly flat road – just mind your toes!

10 POINTS

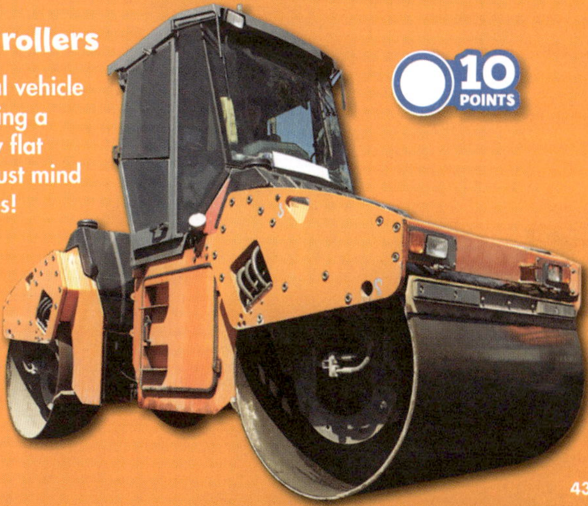

Roadworks

Tipper truck

These huge tipper trucks have very wide tyres so they don't sink into the soft ground.

Lane closure

Part of the motorway has been closed to allow for resurfacing.

Steel piling

Tall piling machines hammer long pieces of steel into the ground to hold back the soil. Some of these girders can be 20 metres under the ground.

Construction workers

Workers must wear high-visibility jackets and hard hats on site.

10 POINTS

Narrow lanes

While repairs and maintenance are taking place there is often limited space so lane width is reduced. Breathe in!

10 POINTS

Roadworks

Wide load

Because lanes are narrower through roadworks, wide loads are asked to straddle both lanes.

15 POINTS

Rejoin main carriageway

Drivers must now stop using the hard shoulder and rejoin the main carriageway.

10 POINTS

Stay in lane

Reduced speed limits usually accompany these signs. Here, it is 50 mph.

10 POINTS

Free recovery

If you break down while travelling through roadworks, a recovery truck will take you to safety for no charge.

15 POINTS

Recovery truck

Major sites have their own recovery truck breakdown vehicles to remove vehicles quickly.

End of road works

At this point, the roadworks are over and drivers may return to a maximum speed of 70 mph.

Bridges and crossings

With over 10 000 miles of motorway, we need many places to cross or go under the motorway – these are just a few.

Motorway bridge

Modern bridges are made from steel and concrete and can be whatever length they need to be.

Other road bridge

There are hundreds of road bridges like this throughout the network.

Suspension bridge

The main cable used in the construction of a suspension bridge is made from thousands of small steel wires.

20 POINTS

Toll bridge

A bridge is expensive to build, so sometimes the government charges drivers to use them.

15 POINTS

Viaduct

A viaduct is a bridge composed of several small stone spans. It was the only construction method available until the use of iron became widespread.

20 POINTS

Tunnel

Sometimes the motorway has to go under a river or through a hill if the environment would suffer too much. Tunnels are very expensive and take a long time to build.

15 POINTS

Bridges and crossings

Footbridge

This footbridge is made of steel and concrete and is arched to add to its strength.

Covered footbridge

This footbridge links services on each side of the motorway and is covered so pedestrians can cross in all weathers.

Cool cars

Ferrari

25 POINTS

Ferrari has been making sports cars since 1947. This Enzo Ferrari has been produced by combining many years of Formula 1 racing experience and technology.

Lamborghini

25 POINTS

Ferrucio Lamborghini started out building tractors before he moved on to the supercars the company builds today. This Murcielago will accelerate from 0 to 60 mph in 3.4 seconds.

Aston Martin

15 POINTS

Aston Martin is a British manufacturer of fast luxury sports cars. The marque is also the perfect choice for special agent 007 James Bond. This is the Aston Martin DB9.

Cool cars

Lotus

Lotus have a reputation for producing cars with outstanding suspension and excellent handling.

15 POINTS

Pagani Zonda

The Pagani Zonda F is an Italian-built lightweight carbon fibre supercar. The secret of the incredible speed of this car lies in its unique aerodynamic design.

40 POINTS

TOP SPOT!

15 POINTS

Porsche

This 911 GT3 has a six-cylinder 3.6 litre engine producing 381 bhp. It can accelerate to 62 mph in 4.5 seconds and has a top speed of 190 mph.

McLaren F1

Once the world's fastest supercar, the McLaren F1 was built with a heavy influence from Formula 1. Only 106 cars were built, so they are very rare. One was sold at auction in London in 2008 for a record £2.53 million.

50 POINTS

TOP SPOT!

Emergency services

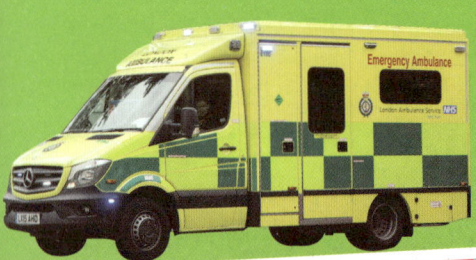

Ambulance

When people need medical help, the ambulance service will arrive as soon as they can.

10 POINTS

Air ambulance

At major incidents, the air ambulance may be called out. It can avoid traffic congestion and uneven road surfaces and fly up to 160 mph. Getting patients to hospital quickly saves lives.

30 POINTS

30 POINTS

Coastguard helicopter

The coastguard helicopter is easy to spot in these distinctive colours.

Fire engine

This fire engine can carry around 2000 litres of water.

15 POINTS

Police motorbike

Police motorcycles are often the first on the scene of an accident, setting up diversions and directing traffic.

15 POINTS

Highways agency vehicle

Motorways are now patrolled by traffic officers as well as police. They clean up after accidents, answer emergency telephones and help motorists.

10 POINTS

Emergency services

Police vehicle with flashing lights

If a police officer sees a traffic offence being committed, they may want to stop the driver by driving up behind with their lights flashing. Or they may need to respond to an emergency, so will use their flashing lights and siren to warn other road users. Other drivers should safely move to one side if a police vehicle with flashing blue lights wishes to pass.

25 POINTS

Police van

Police vans are seen more in city centres than on motorways as they are mainly used to transport large numbers of officers to a location, or to take away citizens that have been involved in a police incident. A rare score for motorway spotters.

40 POINTS

TOP SPOT!

Speed control and cameras

Traffic flow monitor

Traffic flow monitors look for traffic jams and report the data to central control. This information is sent to motorists and receivers can warn them of delays.

5 POINTS

Traffic monitoring cameras

This CCTV camera takes moving pictures for the Highways Agency Regional Control Centre. It enables control centre staff to identify and monitor congestion and incidents.

5 POINTS

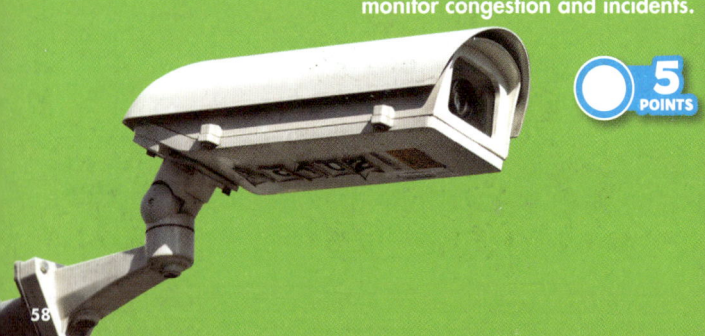

Police van with speed gun

A police speed gun can read how fast a driver is travelling long before they have a chance to slow down.

20 POINTS

Gatso speed cameras

This camera on a fixed pole, made by Gatso, takes pictures of vehicles that are exceeding the speed limit.

 **10 POINTS**

Speed camera sign

This is a warning sign to alert drivers there are speed cameras ahead.

 **5 POINTS**

Leaving the motorway

Exit signs

This is a direction sign on the approach to a junction. They are numbered to help motorists know which exit to take.

5 POINTS

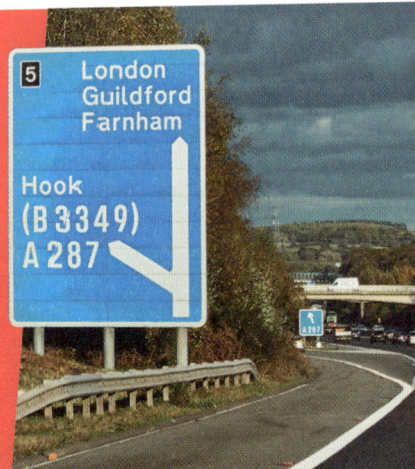

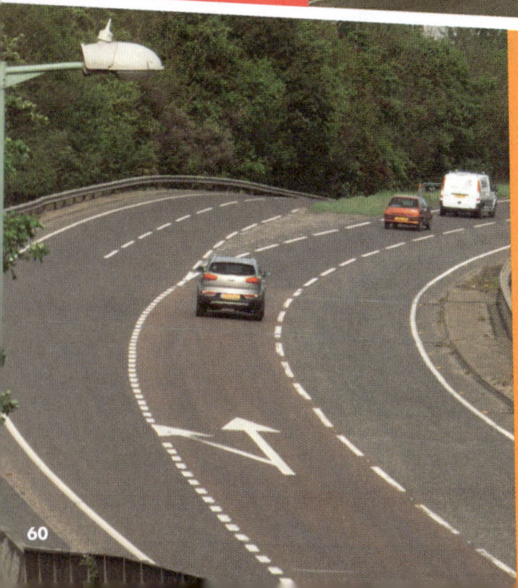

Exit arrow

The arrow painted on the carriageway tells the driver where to leave the motorway.

5 POINTS

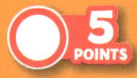

Line in road showing lanes splitting

These lines show where the exit lanes are and should not be driven over except in emergency.

5 POINTS

End of motorway regulations

This informs drivers that motorway regulations stop here.

5 POINTS

Exit slip road

This slip road gives motorists time to slow down safely before the junction.

5 POINTS

Leaving the motorway

Give way sign

This sign tells the driver that he or she does not have right of way and should give way to other motorists at the broken lines.

Local traffic information

These signs give all kinds of information about local road conditions and traffic.

Slippery surface sign

Traffic leaving a motorway and approaching a roundabout could be travelling at high speed and may have to brake hard. Be aware that the surface could be slippery.

Index

100-metrets markers 9
Air ambulance 54
Ambulance 54
Arrow right 41
Aston martin 51
Average speed camera 42
Boat, car towing 22
Box trailer 18
Breakdown recovery 24
Breakdown van 24
Bridge
  Motorway 48
  Road 48
  Suspension 49
  toll 49
Broken down car 27
Caravan, car towing 22
Car park junction 37
Car transporter 18
Castle 35
Cat's eyes 9
Central barrier concrete 9
  Steel 8
Chevrons 5
Children's play area 39
Coach 21
Coastguard helicopter 54
Combine harvester 30
Cones 41
Construction workers 45
Convoy exceptionale 20
Cows 31
Crane 23
Custom car 23
Cutting 28
Delays possible 41
Diggers 45
Embankment 29
End of motorway regulations 61

End of roadworks 47
Exit
  Arrow 60
  Slip road 61
Ferrari 51
Ferry port 33
Fire engine 55
Food bar 38
Football ground 34
Footbridge 50
  covered 50
Free recovery 46
Fuel
  Price sign 40
  Station 40
Gatso speed camera 59
Hard shoulder 7
Hazard
  Biohazard 25
  Compressed gas 25
  Corrosive 25
  Oxidising 25
  Poison 25
  Radiation 25
Highway maintenance vehicle 23
Highways agency vehicle 55
Hot-air balloon 34
Junction 8
Lamborghini 51
Lanes
  Four 6
  joining 5
  Splitting 61
  Three 6
  Two 6
Lane closure 44
Local traffic information 62
Lotus 52
Low-loader 20
Mclaren f1 53
Minibus 21
Motorbike 24
Motorhome 21
Motorway splits 7

Motorways merge from left 7
Narrow lanes 45
No hard shoulder 7
Noise absorbent barrier 29
Outside seating 37
Overhead gantry 26
Oversize load 20
Pagani zonda 52
Parent and child parking 37
People shopping 38
Phone masts 26
Picnic area 38
Pigs 31
Police
  Motorbike 55
  Speed gun 59
  van 57
  Vehicle, flashing lights 56
Ponies 31
Porsche 52
Power station 32
Pylons 32
Railway train 33
Rejoin main carriageway 46
Restaurant 38
Rivers 33
Road markings 5
Road rollers 43
Services 36–40
Sheep 31
Sign
  Airport 12
  Average speed 42
  Blue motorway 4
  Brown tourist 10
  County border 13
  Crosswind 10
  Direction 10
  Distance 12
  Exit 60
  Ferry 12
  Give way 62
  Green primary route 4

No entry 3
Rectangle – information 11
Round – order 11
Services 13, 36
Slippery surface 62
Slow lorries 12
Speed camera 59
Start of motorway 3
Triangle – warning 11
White local route 4
Works access 42
Works unit only 13
Slip road 3
SOS phones 27
Steel piling 44
Stay in lane 46
Street lighting 27
Tollbooths 27
Tractor 30
Traffic
  Flow monitor 58
  Lights 3
  Monitoring cameras 58
Truck,
  Army 19
  Container 17
  Crash protection 26
  Curtain side 18
  Recovery 47
  Tanker 17
  Tipper 44
Truck cab 17
Tunnel 49
Van 22
Variable message signs 14–16
Viaduct 49
Waste bin 39
Wide load 46
Wind turbine 32

63

i-SPY How to get your i-SPY certificate and badge

Let us know when you've become a super-spotter with 1000 points and we'll send you a special certificate and badge!

Here's what to do:

- Ask an adult to check your score.

- Apply for your certificate at www.collins.co.uk/i-SPY (if you are under the age of 13 we'll need a parent or guardian to do this).

- We'll email your certificate and post you a brilliant badge!

WAVERLEY®
SCOTLAND

Tartan Cloth
Commonplace Notebook

If found, please contact:

_____

_____

_____